Resource Pack 1

Understanding community development work

Written by
Dr Val Harris

Contents

Note

To aid your use of this material, pages intended as Tutor Prompt Sheets, Worksheets, Handouts, Case Studies or Reflective Journals have been given an appropriate mark in the top right-hand corners, as shown below.

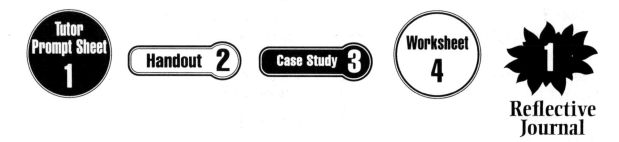

Introduction

This resource pack has been produced by the Federation for Community Development Learning as part of its ongoing commitment to develop and share community development learning practice. The pack is part of a series which is linked to the Open College Network Community Development Programme (see www.fcdl.org.uk or www.syocn.org.uk).

The Programme was developed out of an initial set of courses run by Salford Council for Voluntary Service as part of its community work training programme. The courses were rewritten by Salford CVS and Dr. Val Harris in order to map them to the revised National Occupational Standards for Community Development Work (see www.fcdl.org.uk or www.paulo.org.uk). The Salford units became the first training courses to be mapped to the revised standards in 2002.

The Federation, working with the co-operation of Salford CVS, has accredited the programme through South Yorkshire Open College Network. It has been designed so that further units may be included as and when appropriate. A subsequent set of units has been added to the original list and will be accredited through the OCN Community Development Programme.

The Federation has worked with the Open College Network to develop a National Community Development Award based on this programme. This is the first national community development award that uses the OCN process. It adds to the growing number of qualifications and progression routes for community development workers, managers and activists. For further information on the national award, please contact the Federation or NOCN (www.nocn.org.uk).

A full programme

This resource pack relates to one of the units in the OCN Community Development Programme and can be used to form part of the national award. The programme covers training courses and materials for a range of qualifications levels. To date, these include foundation (1), intermediate (2) and advanced (3) levels. For further information, see the Get Accredited publication produced by the Federation and OCN.

The programme has been endorsed by the England Standards Board for Community Development Work Training and Qualifications. Additional units will continue to be developed and added to the programme.

The full set of units (to be accompanied by resource packs) is listed on the next page.

Level 1

1. Understanding community development work
2. Community development work skills
3. Reflective practice.

Level 2

1. Understanding community development work
2. Community development work skills
3. Effective partnership working
4. Monitoring and evaluation
5. Funding and resources
6. Publicity skills
7. Involving people in community development
8. Planning for community groups
9. Group work skills
10. Developing community organisations
11. Reflective practice
12. Social Justice
13. Identifying needs

14. Neighbourhood regeneration
15. Representing a community of interest/identity
16. Principles into practice.

Level 3

1. Effective partnership working
2. Monitoring and evaluation
3. Funding and resources
4. Publicity skills
5. Involving people in community development
6. Planning for community groups
7. Group work skills
8. Developing community organisations
9. Reflective practice
10. Social Justice
11. Identifying needs
12. Neighbourhood regeneration
13. Representing a community of interest/identity
14. Principles into practice.

Using the resource pack

The packs are written in six blocks of 2-hour sessions so that training sessions can be organised flexibly to meet the needs of participants. They are designed to be run with crêches, in evenings, to fit school times etc., and the 2-hour blocks can be added together.

For each four hours of learning there is one learning outcome so that these blocks can be run as stand alone sessions and people can slowly build up their portfolios if they want to. There are learning journal questions, worksheets, etc., to enable participants to gather evidence of their learning from each session.

Each 2-hour session contains:

◆ A detailed session plan
◆ Tutor prompt sheets
◆ Handouts
◆ Exercises, including case studies, work sheets, role plays, stories and games to support each session.

The pack includes everything you need to run the sessions, however, the materials can be adapted and changed to meet both the trainer's style and the needs of participants. The case studies and other exercises might not be relevant to the participants but do give an example which can be adapted by the trainer.

Developing new resources

The Federation welcomes any feedback and ideas for exercises for the next reprint. This resource pack forms part of a series of publications around community development learning produced by the Federation. For further information, please contact the Federation on 0114 273 9391 or info@fcdl.org.uk

Unit title(s): Understanding Community Development Work

Credit value: One   **Level:** One

Learning Outcome	Assessment criteria	Evidence Number	Assessor	Moderator
The learner will be able to:	**The learner has achieved the outcome because s/he can:**			
1. Understand the key purpose of community development work	1.1 Describe what community development work seeks to achieve			
2. Understand the values and practice principles of community development work	2.1 Describe the main values of community development work and give a practice example for three of the values			
3. Understand the meaning of 'community'	3.1 Comment on the meanings of the word 'community'			
4. Understand power and powerlessness and how it affects people	4.1 Give an examples of the effects of powerlessness on an individual			
5. Understand why people get involved and the barriers to their participation	5.1 Give two examples of why people get involved in community groups and two barriers to their participation			
6. Understand why groups are necessary and the pros and cons of working in groups	6.1 List three benefits and problems of working in groups			

Evidence matrix

Evidence matrix

Unit title(s): Understanding Community Development Work

Credit value: One   **Level:** Two

Learning Outcome	Assessment criteria	Evidence Number	Assessor	Moderator
The learner will be able to:	**The learner has achieved the outcome because s/he can:**			
1. Understand the key purpose of community development work	1.1 Describe the key purpose of community development work and how it applies to an example			
2. Understand the values and practice principles of community development work	2.1 Describe the main values of community development work and relate three practice principles to an example of community work			
3. Understand the different meanings of 'community'	3.1 Describe two different definitions of 'community' and explain their relevance to community work			
4. Understand the terms power and powerlessness and how they affect people and organisations	4.1 Describe the effects of powerlessness on an individual and on community groups			
5. Understand why people get involved in community activities and the barriers to their participation	5.1 Describe the main motivations for people getting involved in community groups and the most common barriers to their participation			
6. Understand why groups are necessary and the pros and cons of collective action	6.1 Describe two advantages and disadvantages of community groups 6.2 Describe how groups help achieve the aims of community development work			

Key purpose of community development work

Key purpose of community development work
Session Plan 1 and 2

◆ **Target audience**

People involved in community activities and community development work

◆ **Length of session**

2 x 2-hour sessions; four hours in all

◆ **Session aim(s)**

To introduce people to the course and explore the key purpose of community development work.

◆ **Session outcomes**

At the end of the session participants will:

● demonstrate their understanding of the key purpose of community development work.

◆ **Indicative content**

● Key purpose statement

● The context of community development work – where does it occur?

● What community development work seeks to achieve – social justice and a fairer world

● Why communities want to bring about changes and how communities can go about it – examples of the range of activities

● Understanding the difference between the community and voluntary sectors; knowing how big and diverse the sector is.

Detailed Session Plan 1

Time	Content	Exercise/Method	Resources	Notes *core topic or optional if time*
0.00	Introductions and domestics	Tutor input	Tutor Info Sheet: Domestic and health and safety checklist	
0.10	Introductory game	Use an appropriate name game for participants to introduce themselves		
0.20	Aims of the course	Tutor input	Tutor prompt sheet 1; put onto acetate or flip chart	
0.25	Ground rules	Pairs to interview each other about their hopes and fears; they feedback each others hopes and fears; then tutor led discussion to agree what groundrules will make the course work for them	Flip chart, pens Tutor prompt sheet 2	Tutor also adds in example, such as 'I worry that no one will come back next week'; so a groundrule about people saying if they are coming or not to a session
0.50	My expectations of the course and what I bring to the course	Individuals to complete the worksheets. Tutor to make list in feedback of skills/knowledge/ expertise that people bring (people to keep the scroll safe)	Worksheet 1 (scroll) Worksheet 2	Worksheet 1 will be referred to again at the end of the course

1

Detailed Session Plan 1

Time	Content	Exercise/Method	Resources	Notes core topic or optional if time
1.05	Where does community development work occur?	Tutor starts by referring to Handout 1. Then whole group to come up with ideas and be recorded on flip chart. Whole group discussion to see if people feel they fit into any of the ideas	Flip chart, pens. Handout 1	
1.30	Key purpose of community development work?	Small Groups – each are given a set of words from the key purpose and asked to arrange into a sentence. Give out Handout 2. Whole group discussion	Key purpose words – slips of words cut out of sheet. Handout 2	
1.55	Ending	If end of session then need to leave 5 mins for ending; if coming back for another 2 hour session after lunch then explain what will be coming next		

Understanding Community Development Work • **Session One**
Federation for Community Development Learning

Domestic checklist

◆ Tell people about:

1. Fire exits and procedures; and if people leave early they should let tutors know so that the register can be amended

2. Toilets

3. Break times and where refreshments are served

4. Smoking areas

◆ Give out any forms

◆ Remember to make a notice for the door.

Aims of the course

To provide an introduction to the occupation of community development work by exploring the issues of:

◆ The key purpose of community development work

◆ The values and practice principles that underlie all good community development work

◆ 'Community' and its different meanings

◆ Power and powerlessness within communities

◆ The motivation of people to become involved in community development activities and the barriers to their full participation

◆ Working with and within groups.

Ground rules

Make a poster with the following points on, read it out at the beginning and check if anyone needs anything else.

Way of working together

◆ We will keep to the start and finish times and the times set by the trainer

◆ All mobile phones to be switched off during the session
(emergency phone number for the centre is ....)

◆ We will respect each other and our different views. We will take care not to offend others by our language and/or behaviour

◆ We will listen carefully to each other and allow people to finish. We will try not to hog the conversation

◆ We will keep personal and organisational information confidential to the group

◆ We can ask for clarification about comments/instructions if necessary.

| Name | Date |

My expectations of the course are

1

2

3

4

5

Understanding Community Development Work • **Session One**
Federation for Community Development Learning

What I can bring to this course

Think about the experience, skills and knowledge that you have gained through life that can be used to help your community. They may come from your home life, work you have done, courses you have been on, activities you have helped out with. Make some notes below and be prepared to share them with the group.

◆ **Relevant experience I can bring**
(for example, of working within groups, communities, etc.)

◆ **Skills that I have**
(people skills, organisational skills, communication skills, managing money and so on)

◆ **Knowledge that I have to share**
(for example, knowledge of my community, of funding sources, of useful contacts, etc.)

Where do we find community development work?

1 Introduction

There is a danger that nearly everyone can say they do community development work; they work in the community, they help people in the community. Community development work is an occupation in its own right; there are national standards which spell out what skills and knowledge people need to be able to undertake community development work. These occupational standards are underpinned by the principles and values previously outlined.

We recognise that there are two basic types of community – there is one based on locality, neighbourhoods, where people tend to live, and another which recognises that people may have common interests no matter where they live, and we talk about them being communities of interests (for example, allotment holders, cyclists in a city or the Hindu community).

2 Community work in action

We would say that community development work is about

◆ Working with others in a community around issues/problems that are clearly defined

◆ Tackling these issues collectively, and in a way that is agreed by the group

◆ Perhaps involving people from outside, as long as their views are not imposed on the group.

This is why we can find people in all sorts of jobs and in unpaid positions (who are not called community development workers) yet who are undertaking community development work. It is also why some people who have titles which would imply that they are community development workers may not be actually undertaking community development work. They may be coming in from outside with their employer's agenda which is not the same as the residents. They may live in an area and have a particular concern but this is not shared by others and they try and 'represent' the community to other organisations when they have no mandate to do this.

At a time when the national government is saying that we need communities to be involved in their own renewal that we need more people to be volunteering and looking after each other, we find that many community development workers no longer have jobs because of local government cutbacks. We also find that they spend so much time trying to get their posts funded that they don't have too much time for doing what they are good at.

Yet community development work is alive and well in all sorts of other places when we start to look around, so here are some examples...

2 In community-based learning, community education, adult education – we can see groups of Asian women, Disabled people, women in Northern Ireland, all coming together to learn and share their experiences and to help each other learn. They are able to take back ideas and skills to other groups they are part of, as well as developing themselves as a group to take the actions they need to improve their situation and their communities.

In community health initiatives – from Health Action Zones where local projects are getting involved, to the development of Healthy Living Centres; sports activities for young people which they run themselves; walking groups for Asian women; tackling poverty through local advice centres; and many other innovative approaches to improve people's health.

In community regeneration and neighbourhood renewal initiatives – but only where local people are actively involved and not just token partners! – so we have examples of New Deal for Communities, local Single Regeneration Budget programmes, community safety initiatives, housing developments and local community enterprises and businesses.

In campaigns – of which there are many to choose from as they range from actions around local traffic problems through to attempts to prevent deportations; tackling racists attacks; working with asylum seekers to change the voucher system; preventing the destruction of habitats for wildlife; and promoting safe walking and cycling routes to schools.

In developing local facilities – such as millennium greens; community allotments; changing empty shops into local learning centres; using the mosques, temples and churches to provide food and socialising for older people; opening community cafes, etc. All of these are aimed at providing places for people to come together to pursue a particular interest which helps to build the networks and links within communities.

There are many other places where we can see community development work in action, where people (paid or not) are trying to build stronger and more inclusive communities. Where we can see:

- communities defining their concerns and issues

- issues being tackled collectively

- use being made of everyone's experiences and knowledge

- issues of power and inequality being tackled

- people actively being involved and encouraged to develop

- the process and the outcome are equally important

- that learning comes through evaluating and reflecting on what has happened so far

...then we are seeing community work in action.

Val Harris

Source: Community Work Skills Manual published by Association of Community Workers and the Community Work Training Company

Key purpose words

(to photocopy and cut out)

The key purpose

of community development work

is collectively to bring about

social change

and justice,

by working with communities to:

identify their needs, opportunities,

rights and responsibilities

plan, organise

and take action

evaluate

the effectiveness

and impact

of the action

all in ways

which challenge oppressions and

tackle inequalities.

The key purpose of community development work

The key purpose of community development work is collectively to bring about social change and justice, by working with communities[1] to:

◆ identify their needs, opportunities, rights and responsibilities

◆ plan, organise and take action

◆ evaluate the effectiveness and impact of the action

all in ways which challenge oppressions and tackle inequalities.

1. 'Communities' refer to those which can be defined geographically or those defined by interest or identity.

Detailed Session Plan 2

Time	Content	Exercise/Method	Resources	Notes *core topic or optional if time*
0.00	Warm up/wake up	Any exercises/games relevant to the time of day		
0.10	What is the difference between the voluntary and community sectors?	Tutor input Worksheet 3 – work in pairs on who is doing what	Handout 3, Definitions, Worksheet 3 Tutor prompt sheet 3	When talking about the difference you may want to give some local examples to highlight the differences
0.40	Why do communities want to bring about changes?	People to draw one aspect of their community that they want to change, and what it would be like if it was changed; put up around the walls and people quickly explain what they want to change	Flip chart, pens	Remind people to just think about one thing – not their entire list of community problems
1.20	Using the idea of community development work – how could we begin to make such changes?	Tutor to recap on key points of key purpose (collective action, identifying needs, opportunities, planning for action....) and then to lead discussion on each picture and make list of ideas using the expertise in the room	Flip charts, pens	
1.35	Open College Network (OCN) Requirements – Registration sheets. Assessments and Portfolio building, Learning Journal questions to be given out	Tutor explanation of requirements and levels	OCN Paper work Learning Journal	Need to get correct paperwork from the OCN you are working with
1.50	Ending game	Choose something to find out how people are at the end of this session, such as relating how they feel to the weather		

Community and voluntary sectors

The National Occupational Standards in Community Development Work define these as:

The Community Sector

The whole range of autonomous collective activity undertaken by neighbourhoods or communities of interest, to improve life and conditions. It is a spectrum which extends from informal activities to more organised community groups.

The Voluntary Sector

The range of groups whose activities are carried out not for profit and which are not public or local authorities. These organisations would normally be formally constituted and employ professional and administrative staff. They may or may not use volunteer help.

…The differences

The differences are often that the groups in the community sector are less formal, have few if any staff, often work with volunteers and on a self-help basis and they are usually locally based. The organisations in the voluntary sector may be bigger and can be providing services on behalf of the local council or health trust; they may be local, regional or national organisations – which may have branches more locally. They are often charities or charitable companies.

There are many more community groups than there are voluntary organisations.

Community development or voluntary sector workers

(Workers can be paid or unpaid)

Which sector do you think each person is involved in? Make a note in the right hand column.

Abdul is a community development worker employed by Barnados

Roger is the Vicar of St Stephen's Church

Arthur is the Chair of the Neighbourhood Watch. He patrols the streets in the evening

Mavis takes the minutes at the Mothers Union

Taj is a local councillor but doesn't live in the ward he represents. He stopped a private developer building on the spare ground near to his house where children play

Sonia works for the local Pre-school Play association running parenting and play classes

Zaira teaches health and diet for the WEA (Workers Education Association – community-based education)

Betty is the chair of the Tenants and Residents Federation for the town

Janet runs a Saturday school for Black youngsters to learn about the history and culture of the West Indies

Shahida is a parent governor for the local primary school

Tony is a volunteer who is working to restore the local cemetery as a wildlife area

Farzana leads 'walking groups' in the local park to help get people fit after a stroke – she is paid a sessional rate by the local GP surgery

Tricia is a volunteer for the local domestic abuse helpline; she answers the helpline two afternoons a week

Yvonne is a worker at the local refuge for women fleeing violence. The lottery fund the refuge and her wages

Ann is a nurse working at the local hospice

Ron organises the van trips to Romania – taking toys and equipment to the orphanages in that country

Amid organises the local Sunday League football team, including practices and getting the players to other matches

Tassy is organising the petition about the chemical spillages from the nearby factory, which have leaked into the local river and spread over the local playing fields

John is a community worker paid by the local community centre to support carers and ensure they receive benefits and services

Becky is a member of a group which promotes breast feeding and runs classes locally to help new mothers

Liz goes along each week to a resource centre to meet new refugees and asylum seekers, to offer friendship and support

Peter is the leading member of a self help group for people who use or have used the mental health services, which campaigns for better services and provides advocacy support to people when dealing with consultants

Karl is a locally elected member of the partnership board for the New Deal for Communities programme for his estate

Chris works for the local Council for Voluntary Service running training courses to support community and voluntary groups in the area

Tariq is employed by the Muslim Welfare Association to raise funds to support overseas projects

Community development or voluntary sector workers

(Workers can be paid or unpaid)

Abdul is a community development worker employed by Barnados

> voluntary sector organisation – could be working in community sector

Roger is the Vicar of St Stephens Church

> voluntary

Arthur is the Chair of the Neighbourhood Watch (NW). He patrols the streets in the evening

> Could be either depending on the way the local group works and how they engage with the community; NW is quite a structured network

Mavis takes the minutes at the Mothers Union

> voluntary

Taj is a local councillor. He stopped a private developer building on the spare ground where the local children play

> Councillors hold formal positions within the public sector; if he has done this within the ward he represents then he would be a public official; if it was outside of the ward he represents he could be described as an activist for tackling an issue near his home and so could be seen as a local activist

Sonia works for the local Pre-school Play association running parenting and play classes

> voluntary

Zaira teaches health and diet for the WEA (Workers Education Association – community-based education)

> voluntary

Betty is the chair of the Tenants and Residents Federation for the town

> community

Janet runs a Saturday school for Black youngsters to learn about the history and culture of the West Indies	community
Shahida is a parent governor for the local primary school	voluntary
Tony is a volunteer who is working to restore the local cemetery as a wildlife area	community
Farzana leads 'walking groups' in the local park to help get people fit after a stroke – she is paid a sessional rate by the local GP surgery	Could be either, depending on how it was set up – did the initiative come from the community?
Tricia is a volunteer for the local domestic abuse helpline; she answers the helpline two afternoons a week	voluntary
Yvonne is a worker at the local refuge for women fleeing domestic violence. The lottery fund the refuge and her wages	voluntary
Ann is a nurse working at the local hospice	voluntary
Ron organises the van trips to Romania – taking toys and equipment to the orphanages in that country	voluntary
Amid organises the local Sunday League football team, including practices and getting the players to other matches	Could be either, as Leagues can be well organised, most likely to be community as that is where it started from
Tassy is organising the petition about the chemical spillages from the nearby factory, which have leaked into the local river and spread over the local playing fields	community
John is a community worker paid by the local community centre to support carers and ensure they receive benefits and services	Could be either, depending on what the focus of his work is; if funded by a larger voluntary organisation or state to give welfare advice and run centre then voluntary is more appropriate; if a small centre and focus is on campaigning and self help to meet local need then could be classed as community

Understanding Community Development Work • **Session Two**
Federation for Community Development Learning

Becky is a member of a group which promotes breast feeding and runs classes locally to help new mothers	Could be either; if a part of La Leche League then its voluntary as bigger organisation; otherwise could be local community initiative around health of children
Liz goes along each week to a resource centre to meet new refugees and asylum seekers to offer friendship and support	community
Peter is the leading member of a self-help group for people who use or have used the mental health services, which campaigns for better services and provides advocacy support to people when dealing with consultants	community
Karl is a locally elected member of the partnership board for the New Deal for Communities programme for his estate	Could be either, depending on who he is representing; should be community if representing local area, but could be voluntary sector representative
Chris works for the local CVS running training courses to support community and voluntary groups in the area	voluntary
Tariq is employed by the Muslim Welfare Association to raise funds to support overseas projects	voluntary

Reflective Journal

To be completed after each 4 hours of group work

Name of participant _____

Name of Tutor/s _____

1 Give a brief description of the topics covered by the group work and highlight your main areas of learning.

2 What did you think and feel about the group? What did you contribute to the group and its work?

3 Did you find anything difficult in the session and/or are there areas you would like us to cover again?

Portfolio question

How would you explain the key purpose of community development work to someone who asked you what it is was all about?

For Level 1 Describe what community development work seeks to achieve (you can describe what your community wants to achieve or refer to some of the examples mentioned in the session.)

For Level 2 Describe the key purpose of community development work and how it applies to an example (either from your own activities or from one raised in the course).

(Complete during the week)

Make notes of anything or thoughts that have occurred during the week which you feel challenged you, or re-emphasised your beliefs/experiences.

Tutor's comments

Signature of participant _____

Signature of tutor/s _____ Date _____

Values and principles of community development work

Values and principles of community development work

Session Plan 3 and 4

◆ **Target audience**

People involved in community activities and community development work

◆ **Length of session**

2 x two-hour sessions; 4 hours in total

◆ **Session aim(s)**

To introduce the values and practice principles of community development work.

◆ **Session outcomes**

At the end of the session participants will:

● demonstrate their understanding of the key purpose of community development work.

◆ **Indicative content**

● The values of community development work

● The practice principles:

▶ Working towards a fairer society

▶ Self determination

▶ Working and learning together

▶ Sustainable communities

▶ Participation

▶ Reflective practice and evaluation.

Detailed Session Plan 3

Time	Content	Exercise/Method	Resources	Notes *core topic or optional if time*
0.00	Welcome back; domestics			
0.05	Warm up exercise – Team building	People Bingo	People Bingo sheets	
0.20	Recap last week; ground rules; collect learning journal	Tutor	Written up groundrules	
0.30	Re-cap on community development by explaining to someone else an example of what you do that is community development	In threes introduce yourself and explain how you are involved in community development. Record key words on a flip chart and feed back to whole group. Tutor to remind people of key purpose statement from last week	Flip chart paper; pens Tutor prompt sheet 4	
0.55	Values of community development	Tutor to explain that community development has its own set of values in the same way as other professions such as doctors. Also that these values have informed community development for a long time	Handout 4 Flip chart, pens, OHP, acetate	Need to emphasis that values are important to community development work

Detailed Session Plan 3

Time	Content	Exercise/Method	Resources	Notes *core topic or optional if time*
1.05	Values and principles we hold	Small groups – Auction	Auction sheets and eight pennies for each group. Tutor prompt sheet 5	
1.40		Whole group discussion		
	Examples of values	Small groups to come up with examples of the values in action; post-it notes and put onto flip charts with prepared headings	Tutor prompt sheet 6 Prepared flip charts	
1.55	End	If end of session then need to leave five minutes for ending; if coming back for another two-hour session after lunch then explain what will be coming next		

People Bingo

The object is to tick all boxes. Go up to ONE PERSON AT A TIME and ask them ONE QUESTION AT A TIME and see if you can tick one of the boxes. Once you have ticked all the boxes shout 'Bingo!'

Someone who came here on public transport	Someone who likes cooking	Someone who has a piercing below the neckline
Someone who likes computer games	Someone who got a good night's sleep last night	Someone who has either bleached, dyed or permed their hair
Someone who likes riding a bike	Someone who can 'roll' their tongue	Someone who does not like chocolate

As soon as someone shouts Bingo, the game ends.

Exercise to recap on community development

Organise the group into threes and ask each person in turn to introduce themselves and say how they are involved in community development. In each three ask them to record the main words/phrases people use to describe their activities.

Before they start the exercise you can remind them of the key purpose statement and model how to introduce yourself in that way. For example if you are a community development work trainer you might explain about helping people to share experiences and learn from each other – so promoting collective working. If you are a community development worker you might explain how you helped with a community profile – so helping groups to identify their needs and opportunities.

Values of community development work

◆ **Social Justice**

Working towards a fairer society that respects civil and human rights and challenges oppression

◆ **Self-determination**

Individuals and groups have the right to identify shared issues and concerns as the starting point for collective action

◆ **Working and Learning together**

Valuing and using the skills, knowledge, experience and diversity within communities to collectively bring about desired changes

◆ **Sustainable Communities**

Empowering communities to develop their independence and autonomy whilst making and maintaining links to the wider society

◆ **Participation**

Everyone has the right to fully participate in the decision-making processes that affect their lives

◆ **Reflective Practice**

Effective community development is informed and enhanced through reflection on action.

Values auction

Give out Handout 5: 'What's it worth' and organise small working groups.
Give each group eight pennies and ask them to allocate to each value

Allow about 10 minutes for their work and then bring them back to the whole group. The whole group discussion often takes quite a bit of time

Summarise by reference back to Handout 4 on the values of community development work.

What's it worth?

What values and principles of community work are important to you?

How much would you put on the values listed below?

How much you would spend on each if you only had 8p to spend?

Also add any extra values and principles that come up during your discussion.

	You spend	Total spend
Everyone has an equal say in deciding about their community		
Creates a better/safer community for everyone		
Provides information, help and support		
Improves community spirit and gets everyone involved		
Helps people get to know each other		
Finds out common concerns of different groups in communities		
Gives people a collective voice		
Values people's abilities and their experiences		
Challenges discrimination and promotes people's rights		
Gets everyone involved in deciding about the community		
Add you values here		
1 _____		
2 _____		
3 _____		

Examples of values

Ask people to return to the groups they were in for the previous exercise. Ask them to come up with at least one example for each of the values based on their own experiences and knowledge.

Prepare flipcharts with the six values headings so that you can note their examples under the appropriate heading during feedback.

It may be easier to take feedback on each value at a time, and get all the groups' examples before moving onto the next value.

Detailed Session Plan 4

Time	Content	Exercise/Method	Resources	Notes core topic or optional if time
0.00	Warm up/wake up	Any relevant to the time of day		
0.15	Practice principles	Tutor to introduce and outline the practice principles and what they are. Small groups to complete worksheet on the case study. Feedback whole group	Handout 6 Case study Worksheet 4 Flip chart, pens	
1.00	Learning from practice – ours and others – to develop sustainable communities	Tutor input on reflective practitioner Small groups – to list and discuss the community groups they know (current and past) and to consider how the practice principles could have sustained their group and overcome barriers to effective community development work. Feedback and tutor to sum up	Tutor prompt sheet 7 OHP, acetate, flip chart, pens. Flip chart, pens. Worksheet 5	
1.45	Any issues about OCN Give out learning journal questions	Tutor to check and answer questions		
1.50	Ending game			

Practice Principles

Social Justice

◆ Respecting and valuing diversity and difference

◆ Challenging oppressive and discriminatory actions and attitudes

◆ Addressing power imbalances between individuals, within groups and society

◆ Committing to pursue civil and human rights for all

◆ Seeking and promoting policy and practices that are just and enhance equality whilst challenging those that are not.

Sustainable Communities

◆ Promoting the empowerment of individuals and communities

◆ Supporting communities to develop their skills to take action

◆ Promoting the development of autonomous and accountable structures

◆ Learning from experiences as a basis for change

◆ Promoting effective collective and collaborative working

◆ Using resources with respect for the environment.

Self-determination

◆ Valuing the concerns or issues that communities identify as their starting points

◆ Raising people's awareness of the range of choices open to them, providing opportunities for discussion of implications of options

◆ Promoting the view that communities do not have the right to oppress other communities

◆ Working with conflict within communities.

Participation

◆ Promoting the participation of individuals and communities, particularly those traditionally marginalised/excluded

◆ Recognising and challenging barriers to full and effective participation

◆ Supporting communities to gain skills to engage in participation

◆ Developing structures that enable communities to participate effectively

◆ Sharing good practice in order to learn from each other.

Working and Learning Together

◆ Demonstrating that collective working is effective

◆ Supporting and developing individuals to contribute effectively to communities

◆ Developing a culture of informed and accountable decision making

◆ Ensuring all perspectives within the community are considered

◆ Sharing good practice in order to learn from each other.

Reflective Practice

◆ Promoting and supporting individual and collective learning through reflection on practice

◆ Changing practice in response to outcomes of reflection

◆ Recognising the constraints and contexts within which community development takes place

◆ Recognising the importance of keeping others informed and updated about the wider context.

For worksheet 4:
Howton Estate – car parking problems

Howton council estate was built in the 1920s as a result of slum clearance in Wendon City, 24 miles away. At the time it had its own rail station, a local pit and an engineering company, but all are now closed. The public transport system is poor and the estate's roads were designed before mass ownership of cars. Car ownership is unusually high to enable local people to get to work and to the services in Wendon.

Car parking is almost all on the street, and is chaotic, with some households owning more than one car. Minor accidents are frequent, and there is concern about children being unable to play out in safety. Funding has recently become available for the renewal of the area and one priority, identified in consultation surveys carried out by the council, has been the need to change the way cars affect people's lives on the estate.

The key community organisation based on the estate is the Howton Tenants and Residents Association (HTRA), which has been involved in the renewal process since it started 12 months ago. At an early stage they decided to focus their energies on a small number of high priority needs as identified by local residents. One of these was about the cars on the estate.

HTRA set up small working groups to look at each priority and work up proposals for action. The group looking at the issue of cars have designed a questionnaire aimed at seeking the views and experiences of all residents whether they were currently car owners or not.

They have followed this up by organising a public event with speakers from the police and local authority, motorist and cyclist organisations, and community representatives from other areas who had taken action on this problem. The group have encouraged non-drivers, cyclists, elderly residents and school students to attend to try and ensure a broad range of experiences and views. About half of the time has been spent in group discussions – perhaps the most interesting being the one where non-drivers explained to car owners how they felt about roads clogged with cars, car noise and smells, and their perception of danger. Car owners have explained their own need for getting to work and to services, their financial contribution to road upkeep, and how safe the estate was in reality.

Whilst there were clear differences of interest, including the feeling of many non-drivers that their views had been totally ignored for years, there was some evidence of minds opening if not changing, and a mutual recognition of the need somehow to find ways of living in the same space amicably.

The group had hoped the event would produce a list of agreed action points to move forward with. In reality this was not possible. More time and more thought were obviously needed.

The HTRA group held an away-day for its own members to take stock of the current position and to look for ways forward. It decided to maintain its efforts to bring the different interest groups together around a series of practical proposals. These included regulated parking together with measures to restrict speed and improve safety, the possibility of setting up a community car repair shop with training, and a longer term commitment to secure better public transport provision. Other proposals for pedestrianised areas, better 'walkways' through the estate and more provision for cyclists would be included. There was general agreement in the group that it was important for the residents themselves to come up with solutions, albeit compromise ones, rather than leave it to the funders and authorities to decide for them.

The group felt its impact would be more effective if its members were more representative, so it began to co-opt people who could represent more fully the different interest groups identified. It also decided to produce a lively newsletter to report its activities and to explore new suggestions. The group organised training sessions to enable residents to speak confidently and effectively at public meetings.

After six months of further meetings a second public event was held; this time without external speakers. The main discussion was around a draft 'Cars in Howton strategy' which, with some changes, was duly adopted by the meeting. The revised strategy formed the basis of a series of demands made to the funders and authorities.

Practice Principles

Which principles can you find being followed in the Howton case study?

Social Justice	Sustainable Communities
Self-determination	Participation
Working and Learning Together	Reflective Practice

Tutor
Prompt Sheet
7

Learning from practice exercise

You can refer to the National Occupational Standards for Community Development Work and explain that one of the key roles of community development work is about helping people to learn from each other. One of the ways that this happens is through reflecting on our own and others' practice.

Explain that as people become more skilled as community development workers they should aim to develop their own reflective practice. This means that they and the groups they are working with, and/or are involved with, should make time to review how they are working especially after each event they undertake. They and the group can look at what worked well, what didn't work well, what they would like to change and what they would do differently in the future.

If you are used to the action-reflection cycle you could use that model – a version which relates to training is included here for you to use and adapt.

The value of learning from reflection and sharing our learning is that we can stop re-inventing the wheel and spend our time more usefully on activities that are likely to prove successful.

The Learning Cycle

Learning through experience

The learning cycle described here is based upon the work of Johnson and Johnson in 1982 and the influence of other writers in the field, such as Kolb. It comprises four essential elements:

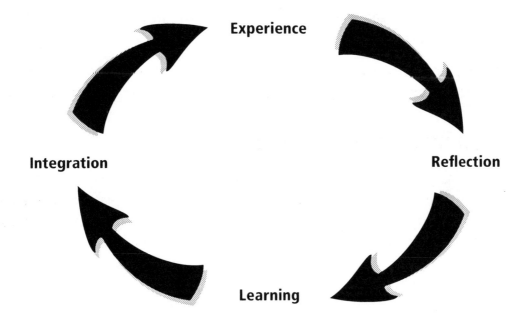

Concrete learning experiences are offered and followed by:

◆ **Observations** and reactions which lead to:

◆ **Reflection** upon what took place, which leads to:

◆ **Learning**; the formation of tentative connections, generalisations, modifications of view and so on, which lead to:

◆ **Longer term influences**; new ideas or connections, which form the basis of new responses to be tested out in future actions and in new experiences.

At their best, participative and experiential methods of learning promote a spirit of interest and enquiry in the individual in a way that transfers to other aspects in life. It thus encourages a more self-directed, self-reliant and self-initiating outlook.

The role of experience

That we all have experiences and that we all learn is a truism. That we can all share an experience, and that we can all learn from it is another. However, we are not all likely to learn the same thing from the shared experience, because each of us will bring to it a personal perspective, a unique value system, and personal preferences that mean we attend to what happens in highly individual and selective ways. This is both the richness and the challenge of experiential methods. This also means the trainer can never be sure that the experience they have designed will communicate the message they intend, or that they can predict with any degree of certainty, what those who take part in it will make of it. And further, whilst we may all learn something from our experiences, we may well overlook useful, or even crucial elements within it, if we do not reflect effectively.

How do individuals repeat experiences time after time, before realising that there is some pattern at work, some element that is influencing this repeated situation, before they can begin to sort it out?

Repetition instead of learning

Experience itself is no guarantee of useful learning. Individuals have to be motivated to learn from their experience and to gain insights into the significance of their experiences for themselves. In a very real sense, the participants are actually generating what they are learning by the quality of the participation they display in the experience they are engaged in and the quality of their reflection upon it.

Community groups: applying the practice principles

In your small group make a list of the community groups that you know of (ideally each person to add one group to the list).

The person who has mentioned a group should briefly describe the community group and to think of a problem that this group had, such as people not coming along. Then your small group should think about which of the practice principles might have been able to help guide the community group to overcome its problems.

You can use the form overleaf to record your group's work.

Name of the community group	Name of the person who talked about it	Nature of the community group's problem	What practice principles might have helped the community groups	Other comments/issues

Reflective Journal

To be completed after each 4 hours of group work

Name of participant _____

Name of Tutor/s _____

1 Give a brief description of the topics covered by the group work and highlight your main areas of learning.

2 What did you think and feel about the group? What did you contribute to the group and its work?

3 Did you find anything difficult in the session and/or are there areas you would like us to cover again?

Portfolio question

What do you understand by the values and practice principles of community development work?

For Level 1 Describe the main values of community development work and give an example of three of the values put into practice.

For Level 2 Describe the main values of community development work. Take three of the practice principles and explain how they affected a piece of community development work.

(Complete during the week)

Make notes of anything or thoughts that have occurred during the week which you feel challenged you, or re-emphasised your beliefs/experiences.

Tutor's comments

Signature of participant _____

Signature of tutor/s _____ Date _____

Understanding of community and gathering information on communities

Understanding of community and gathering information on communities

Session Plan 5 and 6

◆ **Target audience**

People involved in community activities and community development work

◆ **Length of session**

2 x two-hour sessions; 4 hours in total

◆ **Session aim(s)**

To introduce the values and practice principles of community development work.

◆ **Session outcomes**

At the end of the session participants will:

● Demonstrate their understanding of the different meanings of 'community'.

◆ **Indicative content**

● What does the word community mean?

● The importance of understanding your community

● Understanding where their group fits into the wider community

● Knowledge of community networks

● The importance of gathering information on community needs, opportunities, rights and responsibilities

● External and internal factors that impact on communities.

Detailed Session Plan 5

Time	Content	Exercise/Method	Resources	Notes core topic or optional if time
0.00	Welcome; domestics			
0.05	Get to know each other better. Ice breaker – three things about me	Each person to write three things down about themselves – one on each card, and put them in a bag. They then collect a card and have to find the owner. This is repeated three times	Three pieces of card per person Tutor prompt sheet 8	
0.20	Recap last week Collect journals			
0.25	Different definitions/ meanings of community – Locality/Interest and identity	Small groups to discuss the question 'what does community mean to you?' Feedback and discussion. Tutor input on definitions and summarise understandings	Worksheet 6 Flip chart, pens, OHP, acetate	
1.05	Examples of different communities	Small groups to produce a list of the different communities they know about using the different headings and put these onto post-it notes (colour coded)	Flip chart, pens, three different coloured post-it notes. Worksheet 7. Tutor prompt sheet 9	
1.25	How do these fit into the wider community network?	Pin up large scale map of the town/area and ask groups to put their post-it notes on the map to show the range of communities	Tutor prompt sheet 10 Need large scale map of appropriate area/town	If you cannot find a map you could make a sketch of your area
1.55	Summarising	Tutor input on variety of communities to be found in any given area		

Three things about me

Give out three pieces of card to each person and ask them to write a different thing about themselves on each piece of card; collect the cards in and put them into a bag/hat.

Ask people to come and collect one (and if it's one of their own to put it back) they then have to find the owner. When they have made a match, they collect another card and repeat the exercise. When everyone has matched up three people with three pieces of cards, then the game is over.

**In your small group discuss what you each mean by the word 'community'
– what images does it conjure up for you?**

Record your comments here.

Definition of communities

Communities can be defined...

By geography

For example
  by a street,
  an estate,
  a village,
  an area.

By identity

For example
  by disability,
  culture,
  ethnicity,
  sexuality,
  religion.

By interest

For example
  by a leisure interest,
  such as a sport,
  an activity,
  by an interest in the
  environment and
  conservation.

Examples of different communities

You will need sets of three different coloured post-it notes for this exercise; allocate a colour to each of the following and write up on a flip chart:

- **Community of interest**
- **Community of identity**
- **Geographical/locality based community.**

Organise participants into small groups and give out the Worksheet 7 and the three sets of post-it notes.

Ask them to first make a list of the different types of communities they know of, then to decide what type of community they would describe them as. The third column is for any issues they want to bring back to the group.

This exercise leads directly into the next one, so while they are making their lists you should pin up a large scale map of your town/area. The feedback is organised so that people discuss all the communities they have listed and put them on the relevant part of the map.

This should provoke some discussion about the nature of the communities in the area/town. You may need to add in other communities that have not been mentioned, such as small minority ethnic communities, town-wide such as Disabled people or Lesbian Gay and Bisexual (LGB) communities.

Different kinds of communities

In your group complete the grid below.

- Make a list in column A of all the different types of communities you know about
- In column B decide which type of community they are – geographical, interest or identity
- Column C is for your notes during the discussion.

Once you have agreed, write them onto the post-it notes you have been given remembering to use the colour code given by the trainer.

Column A **List of communities**	Column B **What type of community?**	Column C **Comments and notes**

Understanding Community Development Work • **Session Five**
Federation for Community Development Learning

Detailed Session Plan 6

Time	Content	Exercise/Method	Resources	Notes *core topic or optional if time*
0.00	Warm up/wake up	An exercise suitable for the time of day		
0.10	Community networks	Each person to draw a network map of their group and who it relates to. Share maps	Tutor prompt sheet 10	
0.40	What gaps does their group have in their network map?	Small groups/trios to share ideas on what their group wants to achieve and who might be able to help them through the network. Also how could they make the connections?	Tutor prompt sheet 11 Worksheet 8	
1.20	Using networks	How could they use networks to gather information on community needs, opportunities, rights and responsibilities? Either using own situation or case study which focuses on getting to know about external/internal factors that will affect their community	Worksheet 9	
1.45	Ending; learning journals	Evaluation exercise as mid-way – snake or dart board	Tutor prompt sheet 12	

Network maps

Network maps aim to show the links between community groups; they can also include some individual connection. They are a visual tool and so each person needs a large piece of paper and some pens. They start by each person drawing their community group in the centre and then drawing lines out to other groups they have links with. If they have strong links they can make the lines quite strong and thick, if they are quite weak they can make them thinner or dotted.

If people work with several community groups they should just choose one for this exercise. If there are people there from the same organisation/group they should work together on one map for their organisation.

You may find it useful to prepare one for a group you work with/know well to show an example.

The feedback is by people putting their maps on the wall and explaining them.

Filling in the gaps

Once everyone has shared their maps ask people to choose a couple of other people to work with. Each person says one thing that their group wants to achieve which they are not sure how to go about or are finding it hard. The group then looks at their map and suggests other people/organisations that might be able to help them to make progress on this issue.

You will need to circulate and help out with suggestions and encourage people to fill out the bubble sheets of organisations they are interested in but don't have the contacts for and put them on a wall so other people can add in any information.

Worksheet

8

Filling in the gaps in your network

In your small group you need to say one thing that your group wants to achieve but is not sure how to go about it, or that you are finding hard to achieve. Share your map with the other group members and see if they can suggest other contacts of individuals or organisations who may be able to help you. If they do not know the actual contact details fill in one of the balloons and put it on the wall so other people on the course can add in anything they know.

I would like contact details for…

My name is

Using networks

to gather information on community needs, opportunities, rights and responsibilities

1 **As part of the development of a Children's Centre you have been asked about the facilities for child care in your area and whether it is sufficient to meet its needs.**

How would you go about finding out? What groups and networks could you contact to gather this information?

2 **The Local Council has decided as part of its asset management programme to sell off all the publicly owned buildings in the district to the highest bidder.**

How would you go about finding out how this might affect your community? What groups and networks could you contact to gather this information?

Midway evaluation

Suggestions for how to carry this out.

1 **The snake:** draw a long snake which covers two flip chart sheets sideways on, and pin it on a wall. Give all course members several post-its and ask them to write down all the good and not so good bits about the course so far – from the venue, food, group, tutors etc. Ask them to put all the good things above the snake and all the not so good things under the snake.

When all the notes have been placed on the snake you ask everyone to read them.

You summarise the good points and then work through the not so good points and say if and how you will deal with them in the coming weeks.

2 **Dartboard:** draw a dartboard on a flip chart sheet with a large bulls-eye. Bisect the dartboard with lines coming from the bull-eyes to the edge and in each segment put a word on the edge such as venue, tutor, methods.

Give everyone pens and ask them to rate how they think the course is going by drawing dots closer to the bulls-eye if they thought it was good and towards the edge if they think it is not so good.

Again, let people see the result and discuss what needs to be changed.

Reflective Journal

To be completed after each 4 hours of group work

Name of participant _____

Name of Tutor/s _____

1 Give a brief description of the topics covered by the group work and highlight your main areas of learning.

2 What did you think and feel about the group? What did you contribute to the group and its work?

3 Did you find anything difficult in the session and/or are there areas you would like us to cover again?

Portfolio question

How would you describe the community(s) that you are actively involved in?

For Level 1 You should say what you think the word community means.

For Level 2 Describe two different definitions of the word 'community' and explain their relevance to your work/activity in the community.

(Complete during the week)

Make notes of anything or thoughts that have occurred during the week which you feel challenged you, or re-emphasised your beliefs/experiences.

Tutor's comments

Signature of participant _____

Signature of tutor/s _____ Date _____

Opportunities and barriers to community involvement; Understanding issues of power within communities

Opportunities and barriers to community involvement; Understanding issues of power within communities

Session Plan 7 and 8

◆ **Target audience**

People involved in community activities and community development work

◆ **Length of session**

2 x two-hour sessions; 4 hours in total

◆ **Session aim(s)**

To explore issues of power as it relates to community development

◆ **Session outcomes**

At the end of the session participants will:

● Demonstrate an understanding of power and powerlessness and how it affects people and organisations

◆ **Indicative content**

● Power and powerlessness

● Oppression and discrimination

● Different forms of inequalities.

Detailed Session Plan 7

Time	Content	Exercise/Method	Resources	Notes core topic or optional if time
0.00	Welcome, domestics			
0.05	Warm up game: Identity – are people equal?	Everyone is given a role; when a statement is made they step forward if they don't think they will be discriminated against in these situations	Tutor prompt sheet 13 Page with roles cut into slips	
0.15	Different types of inequalities	Put people into pairs to make a picture or list of where their 'role' would encounter discrimination and unequal treatment. Feedback by sharing their pictures/lists in the whole group and general discussion	Tutor prompt sheet 14	
0.45	What creates inequality – the three levels; individual; institutions; society	Tutor input; ask people to think of time when they felt discriminated against and decide which level it came into	Handout 8	

Understanding Community Development Work • **Session Seven**
Federation for Community Development Learning

Detailed Session Plan 7

Time	Content	Exercise/Method	Resources	Notes core topic or optional if time
1.00	Stereotyping and inequality	Organise people into threes; tutor to write up on flip chart the characteristics of a person. The trios write down what their first image is of the person and then to discuss where their images come from. In the feedback ask what they notice first about a person	Tutor prompt sheet 15	
1.30	Understanding different situations	In small groups; decide what level of inequality is taking place in different situations. Tutor to summarise discussion and relate them to many of the issues that community development seeks to tackle and why community development has to work at the different levels	Worksheet 10	
2.00	End			

Understanding Community Development Work • **Session Seven**
Federation for Community Development Learning

Are people equal?

Cut up the role cards and distribute them so everyone has a role.

Line people up against a suitable wall. Explain that they need to be in the role they have been ascribed. Say that 'If you do not face discrimination when doing the following you should take a step forward'.

Going to the cinema

Shopping for clothes

Going on holiday

In employment

Taking out life assurance

Kissing and holding hands with your partner in public

Going into a pub on your own with confidence

Being out on the streets without undue fear of harassment

Finding someone like yourself in a senior management position

Finding positive images of yourself in magazines and on TV.

Once you have worked through this list (and you can add others if you want) ask people to look at where they have got to, share their roles and then move into pairs of their choice for the next exercise.

Role Cards

(To photocopy and cut out)

A 17-year-old male with Down's Syndrome

A 23-year-old heterosexual woman

A 16-year-old mother who is unemployed

An 18-year-old white male with significant visual body piercing

A male single parent with four children under 8

A white wheelchair user

A Black 18-year-old male

A gay man of 45

An unemployed 57-year-old Bengali woman who speaks little English

A 45-year-old white woman who is HIV positive

Understanding inequality

In order to fully understand the idea of equal opportunities, it is helpful to consider the opposite state – that of inequality.

The experience of unequal treatment is often about:

◆   Not being seen or heard

◆   Having your contributions overlooked/devalued

◆   Being limited to roles that are given a low value by society

◆   Never being in the mainstream but always on the edges

◆   Not being allowed to participate in decisions that affect your life

◆   Not being allowed choices

◆   Having little or no economic power

◆   Having your experiences denied or devalued

◆   Being treated as though you have no rights.

These experiences can be caused by unfair discrimination which may occur in different ways.

Understanding different inequalities

When people have paired off from the previous exercise, ask them to remain in the role that they were given and to discuss their situation with their partner.

They are to draw a picture, or make a list, of where they encountered discrimination and unequal treatment. When they have completed this they should return to the main group.

For the feedback ask each pair to introduce their picture/list and then facilitate a discussion about it. You need to bring in the less visible discrimination that occurs, if any of the roles were also deaf, dyslexic, Irish, for example.

Individual/personal

Where one person discriminates unfairly against another because of their own personal prejudices. For example, refusing to have a volunteer with tattoos.

Institution/organisation

Where the organisation unfairly and often unintentionally discriminates against certain people through its practices, policies and procedures. These can operate in:

◆ A formal manner, for example the systems, policies and practices – asking for a degree for a job when it really isn't needed

◆ An informal manner, for example the traditions of the organisation and its styles of working – such as who gets opportunities for training which will help them get a better job in the future.

Society

Where the values held by society endorse the superiority of certain groups over others. For example:

◆ Superiority of men over women, white over black, non-disabled people over Disabled people

◆ The glass ceiling for women trying to get top jobs

◆ Health and Safety regulations being invoked to stop wheelchair users going to the cinema in a group.

Stereotyping

Ask people to get into threes and to sit where they can see the flipchart. Explain that as you write up a situation you want them to note the first images that spring to their minds. Once they have listed them, ask them to discuss where they think that image came from, was it for their own experience, if not where did they get this image from?

The kinds of examples you could use:

◆   An elderly man stood at a bus stop

◆   A young woman pushing a pram along a street with a toddler running alongside

◆   A group of teenagers running towards you

◆   A car full of young Black people with music blaring out as it goes past

◆   A scruffy man sat on a park bench with carrier bags next to him

◆   A group of young Asian women on an anti-war demonstration

◆   A four-wheel-drive vehicle jumping the pedestrian lights as you are about to cross the road

◆   A woman in a wheelchair arguing with a train guard about getting onto a train

◆   A young man working in a day nursery.

At the end of the discussion in the feedback it would be interesting to ask what do they notice about people when they first see them? This can lead to interesting discussions about trainers, jewellery, designer clothing and so forth.

In your group discuss the following situations and decide what kind of inequality is behind each one; is it individual prejudice; institutional discrimination; societal discrimination; or a mixture?

1 An attack on a hostel for asylum seekers

2 The pressure on a gay priest to stand down from being nominated as a bishop

3 The proposal to make all asylum seekers and refugees undergo medical checks

4 Requiring a person to have a licence and a car for a clerical post that is 90% a desk job

5 Requiring a person to hold a degree in order to manage a voluntary organisation

6 The access buses that only run to Sainsbury's and not to Netto

7 An unmarried women paying more for car insurance

8 The number of Black people who get sectioned by the health service as mentally ill

9 The comments on a woman's dress in rape cases

10 Web sites that are not accessible to blind people who use their computers to speak to them (because of all the Flash type of software that cannot be converted into speech)

11 Two women on a bus who are harangued by a man about them being Lesbians and what do they do in bed

12 A Disabled woman standing in a toilet queue and the person next to her asking 'what is wrong with you?'

13 Sending a black-edged condolence card to a mother with a new baby who has Downs Syndrome

14 The proposal that obese people and smokers should pay for their health care

15 People living in an area 'red-lined' by financial institutions, who cannot get credit or bank accounts

16 Victims of crime not being able to get the compensation they are due because the convicted person has not paid the money into the court

17 The 'glass ceiling' that stops women moving into top jobs

18 Women getting paid less than men

19 Refugees with professional qualifications such as doctors and teachers not being able to practice in the UK

20 The lack of men working in childcare and primary education.

Detailed Session Plan 8

Time	Content	Exercise/Method	Resources	Notes *core topic or optional if time*
0.00	Warm up/wake up			
0.10	How does inequality affect your community	Small group discussions. Feedback to create a summary 'map' on flipchart of the key issues affecting communities	Tutor prompt sheet 16	
0.20	Power and powerlessness in/within communities	Small groups to explore what power communities have, and who else might have power	Tutor prompt sheet 17	
0.40	Different types of power	Whole group discussion led by tutor input using Handout 9 and people in group completing Worksheet 11	Handout 9. Worksheet 11	
1.00	Responding to power from external sources	Case studies – small groups to discuss and answer questions. Feedback and discussion	Case study with questions	
1.20	Power issues arising within communities	Role play studies on issues that can arise within a group	Case study – part 2; roles cut up and distributed	It is not important that any decision is made at the role play meeting; it's the dynamics between people with different kinds of power that is important.
1.50	Ending game and learning journals			
2.00	End			

Inequality and community

● **Part 1**

Organise small groups and ask them to produce a summary 'map' on a flip chart of the range of issues which affect their communities which can be related to inequality.

You may want to give some examples, such as poverty, lack of access to services, lack of any say in their own neighbourhoods.

Keep the exercise quite short and fast as it is to set the scene for the discussions in this session.

● **Part 2**

After the feedback use some of the examples that have come up to set the next exercise about power and powerlessness in the community.

Give each group two issues and ask them to discuss what power the community has in this matter, who in the community might have power, and who else might be powerful in this situation.

In the feedback try and highlight:

◆ That communities can have power by making use of opportunities as society changes, for example the government agenda about consultation and participation

◆ But that opportunities to influence can also be diminished, for example, by transferring public services to the private sector.

Different sources of power

There have been many classifications of different types of power. The following list is made up of the most commonly recognised basis of power. These sources of power provide members of community and voluntary organisations with different ways to achieve their goals and of resolving or perpetuating conflict. They also help organisations to work out what power other people and bodies are using to support or frustrate the interests of the community.

Fill in the examples column from your discussions.

Type of power	Examples of it in action
1. Formal authority	
2. Control of scarce resources	
3. Use of organisational structure, rules, and regulations	
4. Control of decision processes	
5. Control of knowledge and information	
6. Control of boundaries	
7. Ability to cope with uncertainty	
8. Control of technology	
9. Interpersonal alliances, networks, and control of 'informal organisations'	
10. Control of counter-organisations	
11. Symbolism and the management of meaning	
12. Gender and the management of gender relations	
13. Structural factors that define the stage of action	
14. The power one already has	

Adapted from Images of organization, Gareth Morgan 1986

Different sources of power

Type of power	Explanation
1. Formal authority	Comes from a place in an organisation that is recognised as powerful – on the basis of individual charismatic qualities; of traditional authority; of bureaucratic position
2. Control of scarce resources	Comes from those who can control the resources such as money, materials, people, technology that others need
3. Use of organisational structure, rules, and regulations	Comes when people can create, change, amend the rules, procedures, and structure of an organisation to increase their power and influence
4. Control of decision processes	Comes when people can influence the outcome of decisions either directly – wheeling and dealing – or by stopping decisions being made in the first place – by keeping control of agendas and not letting some topics get discussed
5. Control of knowledge and information	Comes from controlling who gets to know what and when, making oneself an expert, or from controlling the design of information systems and flows of information
6. Control of boundaries	Those who are the link between organisations, departments; who get to know what is going on and can use that as a lever and who can control access to others (such as, receptionists)
7. Ability to cope with uncertainty	As change is a factor in all organisations those who can cope with it best will gain more power, and may create more uncertainty to keep their power

8. Control of technology	The person/group who can install and maintain technical systems has power through affecting what other people can do (or not)
9. Interpersonal alliances, networks, and control of 'informal organisations'	Comes from friends in high and useful places – to provide information, support, to check out ideas with informally, to swap favours with, to be in the know, to get in first
10. Control of counter-organisations	Getting involved in and taking over those other organisations which can affect what happens to your organisations/group (Trade Unions, pressure groups: for example the hunting lobby attempting to take over the National Trust to stop it banning stag hunting)
11. Symbolism and the management of meaning	Controlling the way that people perceive their best interests, can be directly selling an idea, or by listening and summarising what others have said you can put your own spin on it and subtlety influence their views
12. Gender and the management of gender relations	Gender makes a difference – some people benefit gender relations from the organisational culture which promotes one gender more than another; other people work out a successful strategy to survive within an unfriendly culture, such as women managers who work out the best way to fit in and be seen as credible by male managers
13. Structural factors that define the stage of action	Some people have power from their position – the chief executive – but this can be limited by others who have other types of power and can frustrate the plans of the apparently powerful person
14. The power one already has	Comes from making the most of your power – doing deals with others, calling in favours; energy comes with small victories which encourage people to take on another fight.

External factors affecting a group

A community group established a service for homeless young people by organising overnight accommodation with local families whilst seeking long-term solutions. They had become a registered charity and had succeeded in getting funding from different sources including the local authority. The local authority had agreed a three-year grant to them, as the local authority has to provide services to young homeless people under the government's priorities and they felt this was the easy way to do this. However, after only one year the local authority decided to review its grants system which would affect this arrangement. The councillor responsible for the review's recommendations has agreed to meet the Chair of the Management Committee.

At the meeting the councillor explained that she had been given a budget which meant there was a 30% decrease in the grant funding available. The review group had recommended that in order to be considered for future funding all groups would need to become limited liability companies with charitable status, and to have drawn up 3-year Business Plans which included local authority funding tapering to zero over three years, through a mixture of cost-cutting and income generation.

The Chair commented that these were radical changes and there had been no period of consultation. The councillor responded that it was unfortunate but the real world moves on quickly and any consultation would have been cumbersome and slow. Executive decisions had needed to be made in time for the local authority budgeting process.

The Chair indicated they did not have the technology or skills to comply with the criteria, but did have the commitment to work with local homeless young people. She was offered computers on loan, and incorporation into the local authority accounting system and training.

If the group accepted this position the councillor said then it would most likely continue to receive some local authority funding. However, it definitely would not if the position was not accepted. The councillor then asked for a decision immediately. The Chair insisted that she would need to take this information back to the Management committee for them to discuss.

Questions for group discussion

1 What types of power are being displayed by both characters in this situation?

2 Could either of the characters have used their power in different ways?

Power dynamics within a group

This exercise continues from the previous scenario where the chair of the group had met with the councillor over changes to their funding. The chair has called a meeting to discuss this crisis situation. You are at this meeting and will be given a part to take.

1 **The Chair** (female); you have been with organisation since the beginning as you were one of the founder members. You do not like the scale of change but feel on balance the group has to accept the councillor's proposal to get any funding at all. You don't want to see the group fold and you are prepared to resign over it if necessary. You need to start the meeting by briefly explaining what has happened.

2 **Young person**; you are an ex-user of the service and know its value. You want to keep the service going as it is. You don't think that the Council should dictate how it is organised. You worry about it becoming like all the other council services which have failed young people. You argue to look for other funding to keep the organisation's special ethos.

3 **Committee member** (male); you have only been involved with the group for 18 months and you have a business background. You think the Chair is weak and believe a better deal would have been done if you had been there, rather than what seems to have been a 'cosy chat' between two women. You want to reject deal outright and go back to negotiate on the basis that the Council cannot break its funding contract.

4 **Committee member**; you have only recently joined the committee as a member of the Green Party. You think the group should do the best deal it can now and support the party's plan to stand candidates against the sitting councillors at the forthcoming local elections.

5 **Committee member**; you represent the group on many other committees and you have developed a substantial personal network. You think the group should stall the deal and develop a campaign by contacting everyone in the Council the group knows, to explain your case and lobby meetings.

6 **Committee member**; you are also involved with the local council of voluntary services/voluntary action. You are concerned not just for this service but also for the impact on all voluntary and community groups that are in a similar position. You want the group to work with the local council for voluntary service (CVS) to convene a meeting of all voluntary sector groups affected and develop a campaign against the review.

7 **Committee member**; you are a member of the organisation who provides accommodation to young people and you can see the need to keep the service going. You don't want to get involved in all the politicking.

8 **Committee member**; you work for the council and know the problems they are having trying to balance their budgets. You are worried about the potential job losses in the council and also you want to keep this service going.

9 **Two other committee members** who just want to keep the committee together and focus on the needs of homeless people.

10 **Observers**; the observer's role is to watch as the scenario unfolds and to record the different issues that they can see emerging which are related to the way people are using power to push their point of view.

Reflective Journal

To be completed after each 4 hours of group work

Name of participant _____

Name of tutor/s _____

1 Give a brief description of the topics covered by the group work and highlight your main areas of learning.

2 What did you think and feel about the group? What did you contribute to the group and its work?

3 Did you find anything difficult in the session and/or are there areas you would like us to cover again?

Portfolio question

What kinds of power do you see within your community?

For level 1 Write about an example where an individual might feel powerless; what effect might feeling powerlessness have on an individual?

For level 2 Write about an example where an individual might feel powerless; what effect might feeling powerlessness have on an individual?

Then describe some examples of where community groups might feel powerless and what effect it can have on them.

(Complete during the week)

Make notes of anything or thoughts that have occurred during the week which you feel challenged you, or re-emphasised your beliefs/experiences.

Tutor's comments

Signature of participant _____

Signature of tutor/s _____ Date _____

Session Plan 9 and 10

Involving people in community activities

Involving people in community activities
Session Plan 9 and 10

◆ **Target audience**

People involved in community activities and community development work

◆ **Length of session**

2 x two-hour sessions; 4 hours in total

◆ **Session aim(s)**

To explore the motivation for people's involvement and how to make it possible for them to get involved.

◆ **Session outcomes**

At the end of the session participants will:

● Demonstrate an understanding of why people get involved in community activities and the barriers to their participation.

◆ **Indicative content**

● Consultation and participation

● Encouraging people's involvement

● Who gets involved

● Why do people get involved and who doesn't

● Personal development within community development work.

Detailed Session Plan 9

Time	Content	Exercise/Method	Resources	Notes core topic or optional if time
0.00	Welcome; domestics			
0.05	Warm up game	Personal graffitti	Tutor prompt sheet 17	
0.15	Why people become involved or not	Split into two small groups and ask: 1. What motivates people to get involved? 2. What stops people getting involved? Feedback by groups swapping sheets and adding anything extra	Tutor prompt sheet 18 Flip charts and pens	
0.45	What are we asking people to get involved with?	Whole group exercise to look at the different kinds of community development people can engage with	Tutor prompt sheet 19 Prepared flip chart	
1.05	Who needs to be involved?	Small groups to complete case studies using the worksheet. Each group to take one of the examples and answer the questions. Feedback and discussion	Worksheet 12	
2.00	End			

Understanding Community Development Work • **Session Nine**
Federation for Community Development Learning

Personal graffiti

◆ **Aim**

Get the group to relax and chat to each other

◆ **Materials**

Large piece of paper; felt tip pens

◆ **Time**

10 – 15 minutes

◆ **What to do**

● Lay the paper on a table and hand out the pens

● Ask everyone to find an object they usually carry with them that might be important to them in some way, such as a diary, watch, credit card, etc.

● They place their object on the paper, draw round it and sign their name

● Each person in turn then picks up their object, says what it is and why it is important to them.

◆ **Comments**

Might not suit large groups

◆ **Variations**

You could take unusual objects and let the group try to guess what they are

What motivates people?

The purpose of this exercise is to get participants to think about people's motivation. Encourage them to start with their own motivation and that of people they know.

We often hear about people and communities being apathetic. We need to demolish this myth as there are millions of people who are active in the community and voluntary sectors*. We want participants to identify why people may not be coming forward.

This exercise requires you to split the group into two, both with pens and flip chart papers. Ask each group to look at what motivates people to get involved and what stops them getting involved.

When each group has finished ask them to swap sheets and add in anything else that is missing. You can then summarise key points.

see over for some facts that might convince the sceptics

Reasons to be cheerful about involvement

Someone is bound to bring up the notion that communities are apathetic and most don't want to be involved. You may want to explore this by raising the following points:

◆ If people are apathetic, why are so many new charities registered every year? In the year before March 2000 the Charity Commission dealt with over 8000 registration applications; it approved 5,400 and in the year before it had approved nearly 6000

◆ There are 185,948 charities on the Register (of which 161,200 are 'main' charities; the remainder are subsidiaries or branches of other charities)

◆ There are an estimated 1.1 million charity trustees – all unpaid

◆ It is estimated that unpaid charitable work in relation to direct service activities is valued at over £8.1 billion, fund-raising £6.6 billion, and administration £790 million

◆ The Centre for Volunteering estimates that there are 22 million adults involved in formal volunteering each year and that 90 million hours of formal voluntary work takes place each week

◆ Why did 1.5 million people turn out for a demonstration in February 2003 against the recent war on Iraq?

◆ Why are local papers full of stories about people campaigning about threats to their communities – from chemical plants, house building on green belt to school closures.

The main reason people don't engage with the formal structures and attempts by many councils is that:

◆ They know they are tokenistic

◆ The councils are only going through the motions

◆ Whatever they say won't make any difference

◆ Public meetings are held at times it's hard to get to, without child care support, and run in a way it's hard for anyone to speak up or get listened to

And so forth.

There are many examples all around the country and the world where people are standing up for their communities. Current examples can be found in magazines such as the New Internationalist, Red Pepper, Guardian Society (Wednesday's paper) and look in local newspapers.

What are people getting involved in?

In this exercise we are looking at the range of opportunities that there are for people to become involved in community development, different activities will attract different people. Divide a flipchart into two columns, and make a list of opportunities available in the first column and leave the second one blank.

The kinds of opportunities could include:

◆ Joining a campaign to save the local school playing field from being sold off for housing

◆ Joining the management committee of a local community centre

◆ Representing the Lesbian, Gay and Bisexual community on a local regeneration partnership

◆ Becoming involved in the local neighbourhood watch

◆ Attending area panel meetings

◆ Starting a group to get safe routes to schools for children – either through cycling or a walking bus

◆ Volunteering to fund-raise for books/videos for the Saturday school for Black children of Caribbean descent

◆ Representing the community care alliance on the meetings about commissioning services for Disabled people

◆ Reading the local paper to see if anything is happening that will affect your area

◆ Helping out at the local playgroup one session a week

◆ Starting up a community business.

In the whole group ask the question – who might be interested/motivated to get involved in each of these?

Then talk a little about the different levels that people can engage in community development:

◆ Raising new issues and bringing people together

◆ Running short-term campaigns

◆ Getting directly involved in providing a service

◆ Supporting local groups through fund-raising

◆ Managing local groups

◆ Starting up a new enterprise

◆ Contributing to community consultations

◆ Representing their community – geographical or of interest.

Getting people involved

1 **The local regeneration partnership wants to involve more young people in planning for their areas and getting their interests represented. They like the ideas of youth partnerships or a youth parliament.**

Who would need to be involved in developing these ideas?

What practical steps would need to be taken to encourage people to become involved and to maintain their involvement?

2 **The local resource centre wants to develop the range of training/learning opportunities it can offer to people living nearby; it currently offers woodworking, arts and crafts and computer skills. It intends to apply for local regeneration funding but needs to show that it has engaged the community in planning its new services.**

Who would need to be involved in developing these ideas?

What practical steps would need to be taken to encourage people to become involved and to maintain their involvement?

3 The local council has decided that it wants Neighbourhood Action Plans developing for its most deprived area – which is an area a mile or so from the centre. It is a very poor area with more than thirty different cultural and minority ethnic groups. It expects people to come together in an area and bid for the first small grant to help it develop the plan, and then to bid again for more money to put the plan into action.

Who would need to be involved in developing these ideas?

What practical steps would need to be taken to encourage people to become involved and to maintain their involvement?

4 The local council has been required by central government to establish children's centres in its most deprived areas. It chooses to do this by establishing a partnership group of all the main agencies and researching where existing provision could be adapted to meet the criteria for Children's Centres. In one area it realises that it will need to start from scratch as nothing exists.

Who would need to be involved in developing these ideas?

What practical steps would need to be taken to encourage people to become involved and to maintain their involvement?

Detailed Session Plan 10

Time	Content	Exercise/Method	Resources	Notes core topic or optional if time
0.00	Warm up/wake up			
0.15	Encouraging people's involvement	What can people get from being involved? Small groups to produce material for checklists	Tutor prompt sheet 20 Post-it notes	
0.35	Involving minority communities	Speaker from a minority community who can talk about the development of a community and how this has led to their involvement in wider community events/ issues	Need to organise a speaker from your local area	
1.10	Techniques for involving people	Display of different methods other than public meetings	Tutor prompt sheet 21 Examples which use visual material such as parish maps, visits, shadowing and mentoring	Explain that there is a three-hour session just on this and a full course on this topic if they are interested
	Ending game; learning journals			
2.00	End			

The benefits to people of being involved in community

Start by reminding people about the last session, about why people become involved, and ways to encourage their involvement. Then begin to talk about the benefits of people becoming involved – what is in it for them? It is well known that doing voluntary work can lead to people getting jobs, but what about being involved in community development?

Divide people into small groups and give them post-it notes; ask them to think about what they have gained from being involved and what they think people could gain. You could refer to the key role of working together and learning from each other as a starting point.

Collect their post-it notes and group them together to make a checklist which could be used by them in future to encourage people to become involved.

Techniques for involving people

The aim of this slot is to introduce people to the idea that the best way to involve people is rarely through public meetings. This is intended as a taster session to encourage them to look in more depth at this topic and to signpost them to the 3-hour taster session or to the other OCN units. *

Ask the group how they became involved and note these on a flip chart.

Talk about different ways that might engage people's interest such as parish/area maps; planning for real; round table workshops; speak out events.

You can use some of the ideas from such sources as:

◆ Tony Gibson's *Power in Our Hands* 1996, Jon Carpenter Publishing

◆ *Shell Better Britain Campaign* – interactive newsletter and web site www.sbbc.co.uk

◆ *What a Difference Pack,* Dorset Community Action, telephone: 01305 216413

◆ *Groundswell Toolkit for Change* www.groundswell.org.uk

◆ *Participation Works – 21 techniques of community participation;* New Economics Foundation.

It would be more effective if you could show that such techniques have been used in similar situations or in nearby areas. This might affect your choice of examples.

As well as some of these ways of engaging lots of people, you could also talk about how people can get involved through individual mentoring and shadowing opportunities, to get a real feel for what is happening and how they could get involved.

*See www.fcdl.org.uk or phone Federation for Community Development Learning on 0114 273 9391

Reflective Journal

To be completed after each 4 hours of group work

Name of participant

| Name of tutor/s |

1 Give a brief description of the topics covered by the group work and highlight your main areas of learning.

2 What did you think and feel about the group? What did you contribute to the group and its work?

3 Did you find anything difficult in the session and/or are there areas you would like us to cover again?

Portfolio question

For level 1 Describe two examples of where people have got, or might get, involved in community groups, and say why they did.

Think of two barriers that would stop other people getting involved.

For level 2 What do you think are the main motivators for getting people involved in community activities? – give some examples.

What are the most common barriers that affect people's participation in community development activities?

(Complete during the week)

Make notes of anything or thoughts that have occurred during the week which you feel challenged you, or re-emphasised your beliefs/experiences.

Tutor's comments

Signature of participant _____

Signature of tutor/s _____ Date _____

Collective action and our journey so far

Collective action and our journey so far
Session Plan 11 and 12

◆ **Target audience**

People involved in community activities and community development work

◆ **Length of session**

2 x two-hour sessions; 4 hours in total

◆ **Session aim(s)**

To explore the effectiveness of collective action and decision-making.

◆ **Session outcomes**

At the end of the session participants will:

- Demonstrate an understanding of why groups are necessary and the pros and cons of collective action.

◆ **Indicative content**

- The power of collective action

- Strengths and weaknesses of collective action

- Identifying aims and objectives for collective action

- Collective decision making

- Why groups are necessary

- Strengths and weakness of groups/networks

- Co-operative practices within groups.

Detailed Session Plan 11

Time	Content	Exercise/Method	Resources	**Notes** *core topic or optional if time*
0.00	Welcome; domestics			
0.05	Warm-up exercise	The sun shines on – or similar lively exercise for the last day	Tutor prompt sheet 22	
0.15	Collective action in community development	Tutor input on what we mean by collective action; referring back to the key purpose. Groups to consider the pros and cons of collective action and give some examples of each	Tutor prompt sheet 23 Worksheet 13	
0.45	Identifying aims and objectives for collective action	Tutor input on aims/objectives. Small groups to prepare the aims and objectives for a campaign	Tutor prompt sheet 24 Handout 10 Worksheet 14	
1.40	The role of groups in community development	Whole group discussion on 'If we didn't have groups as we know them what would we need to invent?'	Tutor to lead quite a light hearted discussion to bring together the topics covered this session	
2.00	End			

The sun shines on

◆ **Aim**

To get people physically moving around – good when energy levels are low

◆ **Materials**

Chairs in a circle

◆ **Time**

5 – 10 minutes, or as long as people can keep going

◆ **What to do**

- Place the chairs in a close circle with no gaps – one less than the number of people in the group

- Stand in the middle and make a statement like 'The sun shines on everyone with black shoes' – you must have the characteristic yourself

- Everyone with black shoes has to get up and find another chair, and you get into a chair

- The person left standing does the next 'The sun shines on…', and so on

◆ **Comments**

- Not suited for people with mobility or visual impairments

- Make sure the person in the middle chooses something they can move to, or they get 'stuck'

Collective action

The purpose of this input is to ensure that participants have grasped that community development work is essentially about working together to achieve change. That it is not just about individuals attempting to do something for their community or about public services provided to individuals in a group setting, such as a group home for Learning Disabled people run by the local council or big charity.

You can refer back to the first session and Handout 2 on the key purpose of community development work.

You can then talk about collective action coming in different forms; for some examples:

◆ A group is set up

◆ Alliances are built around a campaign

◆ Networking is carried out to share information and support activities of other organisation

◆ An e-mail campaign is organised

◆ Demonstration.

Flip chart these ideas and ask the group for other forms of collective action.

Divide participants into small groups and give a couple of the forms of collective action to each group and ask them to think of the pros and cons of each one and to come up with examples if they can. Use Worksheet 13.

In the Feedback, pull out the general pros and cons of collective action which could apply to all its forms.

Collective action

 Write in one of the forms of collective action you have been given

What are the pros and cons of this approach?

The pros	The cons

Can you think of any examples of this kind of collective action?

2 Write in the other form of collective action you have been given

What are the pros and cons of this approach?

The pros	The cons

Can you think of any examples of this kind of collective action?

Identifying aims and outcomes for collective action

Using Handout 10, or another way of identifying aims and outcomes for collective action that might be more relevant. Discuss how a group identify aims and objectives.

Divide participants into small groups and give them an example of potential collective action, either from the list below or other topical ones in your area. Ask them to determine the aims and outcomes.

◆ Making the streets safe for children going to and from the local primary school and for them to be able to play in them after school, at weekends, and holidays

◆ Getting the access bus (run by one of the large private bus companies – paid for by local council) for disabled people to go to the cheaper supermarkets and not just the expensive ones

◆ Preventing the private developers who have taken over the council housing from knocking down your street of houses and relocating you and your neighbours anywhere else while they build houses for sale on the site

◆ Ensuring that the local allotments are better used so that the land isn't sold off to developers

◆ Organising a campaign to keep open a post office on an estate with many older people which is threatened with closure. It will be replaced by a counter in the large supermarket a couple of miles away which is not on a direct bus route

◆ Improving the local park which is being neglected. The play equipment is vandalised and not replaced, the bushes are overgrown and minimal maintenance is carried out. It is the only green space for children to play and people to walk their dogs in the area, and it is beginning to feel unsafe and a no-go area.

Aims and outcomes for collective action

The Community Development Foundation in its 'Gaining Ground Support Pack for Community Groups' has the following definitions:

Aims provide the purpose of the group/network, etc, and the impact it wants to have. For example:

◆ To improve the quality of life of older people on our estate

◆ To empower older people to have greater control over their lives.

Objectives are about how the group/network is going to meet its aims – the stepping stones. These should be achievable and practical. For example:

◆ To run an older persons' social club

◆ To involve older people in making decisions about the running of the club

◆ To work with older people to increase the take-up of their benefits and rights

◆ To support campaigns initiated by older people to protect local facilities and benefits.

You have been given a case study; in your group decide on the aims and objectives of a collective approach to the issue.

Case study on:

Our aims:

Our objectives:

Understanding Community Development Work • **Session Eleven**
Federation for Community Development Learning

Detailed Session Plan 12

Time	Content	Exercise/Method	Resources	Notes *core topic or optional if time*
0.00	Warm up; domestics	Our journey so far…	Tutor prompt sheet 25	
0.10	Example of a local group	Input about a group they were involved with which sort of worked but could have been better	This could be by the tutor, members of the group or an external speaker	
0.30	Draw out strengths and weaknesses and what could be done differently	Small groups to discuss the example and make suggestions	Flip charts, pens	
1.00	Quiz	Quiz sheet given out. Small teams do quiz like a 'pub' quiz and then swop and mark each others	Handout 11: quiz sheet	
1.10	Ending arrangements; portfolios, etc.	Tutor input. Questions and answers		
1.25	Evaluation of course	Can be both a visual evaluation and a written one if needed by funders		
1.40	Ending game	Positive posters	Handout 12: Everyone to have a sheet and put name in box; put sheets on table and people make a positive comments on each person's sheet	
2.00	End			

Our journey so far

Ask members of the group to reflect about the course as a whole and to think about how they could describe it in terms of a journey.

You could start by describing your journey to give an idea of how long or short to make the statement and to give people thinking time. Ask the group to share their journey when they are ready. Make sure everyone has the chance to say their story.

Understanding community development work: quick quiz

Team name	Team members

1 What is the aim of community development work?

2 Name three 'powerful' groups in society

3 Name three 'powerless' groups in society

4 Give two reasons why group work is more effective than working on your own

5 What is the key purpose of community development work?

6 Name three values in community development work

7 Give three examples of where using these values in practice would positively change things for individuals and communities

8 Name two different types of community

9 Give two effects that being 'powerful' would have on a person

10 Give two effects that being 'powerless' would have on a group

11 Give two reasons why people don't join groups

12 Give three reasons why people do join groups

13 Give two advantages of being a community group

14 Give two disadvantages of being a community group

15 Name three items you could use as evidence in a portfolio.

What's good about me

This is your positive poster

Reflective Journal

To be completed after each 4 hours of group work

Name of participant _____

Name of tutor/s _____

---

1 Give a brief description of the topics covered by the group work and highlight your main areas of learning.

2 What did you think and feel about the group? What did you contribute to the group and its work?

3 Did you find anything difficult in the session and/or are there areas you would like us to cover again?

Portfolio question

Why are groups important in community development?

For Level 1 Give three examples of the benefits of working in groups, and briefly describe three problems that can arise.

For Level 2 Describe, with examples, two advantages and two disadvantages of community groups. Describe, with examples, how groups can help achieve the aims of community development work.

(Complete during the week)

Make notes of anything or thoughts that have occurred during the week which you feel challenged you, or re-emphasised your beliefs/experiences.

Tutor's comments

Signature of participant _____

Signature of tutor/s _____ Date _____